# The British Raj: The History and L[ India and the In

The British Raj's flag

# About Charles River Editors

**Charles River Editors** is a boutique digital publishing company, specializing in bringing history back to life with educational and engaging books on a wide range of topics. Keep up to date with our new and free offerings with this 5 second sign up on our weekly mailing list, and visit Our Kindle Author Page to see other recently published Kindle titles.

We make these books for you and always want to know our readers' opinions, so we encourage you to leave reviews and look forward to publishing new and exciting titles each week.

# Introduction

**A depiction of the Queen's Own Madras Sappers and Miners, 1896**

## The British Raj

"A significant fact which stands out is that those parts of India which have been longest under British rule are the poorest today. Indeed some kind of chart might be drawn up to indicate the close connection between length of British rule and progressive growth of poverty." - Jawaharlal Nehru, *The Discovery of India*

The British East India Company served as one of the key players in the formation of the British Empire. From its origins as a trading company struggling to keep up with its superior Dutch, Portuguese, and Spanish competitors to its tenure as the ruling authority of the Indian subcontinent to its eventual hubristic downfall, the East India Company serves as a lens through which to explore the much larger economic and social forces that shaped the formation of a global British Empire. As a private company that became a non-state global power in its own right, the East India Company also serves as a cautionary tale all too relevant to the modern world's current political and economic situation.

On its most basic level, the East India Company played an essential part in the development of long-distance trade between Britain and Asia. The trade in textiles, ceramics, tea, and other goods brought a huge influx of capital into the British economy. This not only fueled the Industrial Revolution, but also created a demand for luxury items amongst the middle classes.

The economic growth provided by the East India Company was one factor in Britain's ascendancy from a middling regional power to the most powerful nation on the planet. The profits generated by the East India Company also created incentive for other European powers to follow its lead, which led to three centuries of competition for colonies around the world. This process went well beyond Asia to affect most of the planet, including Africa and the Middle East.

Beyond its obvious influence in areas like trade and commerce, the East India Company also served as a point of cultural contact between Western Europeans, South Asians, and East Asians. Quintessentially British practices such as tea drinking were made possible by East India Company trade. The products and cultural practices traveling back and forth on East India Company ships from one continent to another also reconfigured the way societies around the globe viewed sexuality, gender, class, and labor. On a much darker level, the East India Company fueled white supremacy and European concepts of Orientalism.

Ultimately, the company's activity across the Indian subcontinent led to further British involvement there, and the British Raj, a period of British dominance and rule over India that formally began in 1857 and lasted until 1947, remains a highly debated topic amongst historians, political scientists, the British people, and the people of modern India. In Martin Deming Lewis's *British in India: Imperialism or Trusteeship*, he attempts to settle the question, opening with opposing views of those closest to British India:

> "No romance can compare with the story of the handful of Englishmen . . . who, beginning as mere traders and merchant settlers, have in barely two centuries built up the majestic structure of an Imperial system under which peace, order and good government are secured for three hundred and fifty millions of human beings inhabiting what is in essence a continent of its own." - A 1942 Raj official

> "Those parts of India which have been longest under British rule are the poorest today. . . Nearly all our major problems today have grown up during British rule and as a direct result of British policy: the princes; the minority problem; various vested interests, foreign and Indian; the lack of industry and the neglect of agriculture; the extreme backwardness in the social services; and, above all, the tragic poverty of the people." -Jawaharal Nehru, imprisoned Indian reformer, 1944

How can it be that two contemporaries view the same phenomenon so differently? Without a full understanding of the Raj, simplifications and hastily-drawn conclusions are the only possible outcomes. Instead, it's necessary to seek an understanding of the people, forces, and events shaping the history of British India to arrive at valid conclusions about the British-Indian experience and to understand the continued divide over its legacy. Perhaps then it's possible to answer Lewis's question: "Is it possible that British rule was both destructive and creative at the same time?"[1]

*The British Raj: The History and Legacy of Great Britain's Imperialism in India and the Indian Subcontinent* looks at the importance of British colonialism in the region, and how it has affected the course of history to this day. Along with pictures and a bibliography, you will learn about the British Raj like never before.

---

[1] Martin Deming Lewis, ed., British in India: Imperialism or Trusteeship? (Boston: D.C. Heath, 1962), vii.

**Prelude to the Raj: The Dominance of the British East India Company**

**Sir Charles Wood (1800–1885) was President of the Board of Control of the East India Company from 1852 to 1855; he shaped British education policy in India, and was Secretary of State for India 1859–66.**

Europeans had been seeking Asian spices, silks, and other goods since at least the Middle Ages. Prior to the early modern period, most of these products had to be transported along the Silk Road connecting China to South Asia and Europe. While trade between these regions existed, it was at a smaller scale compared to the trade within and between the major Asian empires. This was largely due to the relatively poor nature of European goods; European civilizations simply did not produce anything of comparable value to Asian goods. In addition, transporting goods across land meant that each commodity changed hands several times between

East Asia and its eventual European consumer; as a result, only the wealthiest members of European society could afford to purchase items like silk and pepper (Blaut, *Colonizer's Model*).

This imbalance in commodities and resources changed with the European colonization of North and South America. In South America, the Spanish found enormous quantities of silver in the Bolivian mines of Potosi. The silver bullion and other mineral wealth harvested from the conquest of the New World finally gave European nations a trading commodity that appealed to merchants and rulers in Asia. The introduction of Bolivian silver into the global economy followed quickly on the heels of expeditions such as Vasco da Gama's rounding of the Cape of Good Hope, which allowed for travel to Asia by sea instead of by land. These two factors together provided the catalyst for renewed European interest in Asian trade (See Stein, *Silver, Trade, and War,* 52). Despite increased mobility and access to resources, long-distance trade between Europe and Asia remained extremely dangerous and expensive in the 17th and 18th centuries. As it was rarely feasible for an individual merchant or small merchant company to undertake the journey, a new form of organization emerged, the joint stock company.

The British East India Company was founded in 1600 by several London merchants through a Royal Charter from Queen Elizabeth I. The Dutch East India Company (VOC), which formed almost simultaneously, quickly had considerable successes bringing goods from Asia to Europe, while the Spanish had by far the greatest foothold in the New World and the Portuguese had been at the forefront of African and Asian exploration. Essentially, the East India Company emerged at a moment when the British appeared to be at a disadvantage compared to their European rivals.

It is also important to note that despite its later significance in the formation of the British Empire, the East India Company did not initially form with colonialist motives. At its start, it focused strictly on trade by means of establishing outposts in overseas ports, forming trading partnerships with local merchants, and cornering the market on profitable goods in particular regions (Marshall, "British in Asia," 490-91). The East India Company formed during a period when similar ventures were being formed for other parts of the world; trading companies sought profits in British North America, the Pacific, and South America. While other ventures initially had more success, the East India Company eventually became the most profitable and influential.

In the 1600s, India was open to a number of foreign traders and had agreements, not only with the British but also the Dutch, the French, and the Portuguese. In fact, it was partially in the interest of Indian leaders, such as Mughal emperor Jahangir[2], to invite the British into a closer relationship with India to counter the influences of the proselytizing Catholic Portuguese.

Although it was technically a private company rather than an organ of the British state, in some ways Britain's East India Company operated like its own country, including engaging in such

---

[2] Ian St. John, The Making of the Raj: India under the East India Company (Santa Barbara, CA: Praeger, 2012), 3.

practices as diplomacy and having its own armed forces. In other ways, however, it was very much a business enterprise, the central concern of which was profit. These two functions and their goals were sometimes directly opposed to each other; maximizing profits could lead to starvation and rebellion, while effective governance sometimes meant taking less profitable measures. This tension was constantly at work not only in India but in the interactions between the British Crown, the Court of Directors who dictated major decisions in India, and the people on the ground there.

The British East India Company sought a number of Indian products for export to the homeland or other British colonial destinations, including cloth, silk, indigo, saltpeter, and spices like pepper and cardamom."[3] Thus, at the beginning, "the relationship between Indians and Britons was a purely commercial one. The impact of the British on the cultural life of India was marginal and neither side could have anticipated that this handful of traders would come to dominate the subcontinent."[4]

It was, according to many traditional British historians, the decline of India that led to her initial subjugation. Percival Spear, professor and author of multiple works on Indian history, asserted that when the officers of the British East India Company began arriving in India, they "found a country in ruins…Not only did they encounter dismantled fortresses and deserted palaces, but canals run dry, tanks or reservoirs broken, roads neglected, towns in decay, and whole regions depopulated…India was exhausted and for the moment without inspiration… Everywhere the links between the rulers and the people had been snapped…The rule of force was universal and politically there was no hope."[5]

Many modern writers and commentators, however, rail against the idea that India was in need of British aid, or that India was even in a state of decline to begin with, calling these claims "inadequate and self-serving."[6] Instead, they argue the British historically disguised their imperial designs on the country as necessary and humanitarian interventions. Ian St. John, though an apologist for this view, cautions against a simplistic interpretation of the British role in the eventual subjugation of India. The Raj, he claims, "that ultimately emerged was neither planned nor envisaged at the commencement of the process. Any suggestion that the East India Company would come to occupy the imperial throne vacated by the Great Mughal would have appeared outlandish to Britons and Indians alike."[7]

St. John also argues that it is important to understand that the Raj, rather than something that happened to Indians, was a phenomenon brought on by the operation and even design of particular Indian sub-groups; that "Important sections of Indian society have as fair claim to be

---

[3] Ibid., 11.
[4] Ibid., 4.
[5] Ibid., 8.
[6] Ibid.
[7] Ibid., 10.

considered the architects of the Raj as the British themselves."[8]

Moreover, for the first hundred years of its existence, the East India Company could hardly be considered a resounding success. It quickly landed in India and signed its first treaty with the Mughal Dynasty in 1615, securing the right to trade from a factory in Surat (Timeline). From there, they traded in textiles, indigo, cotton, and saltpeter, the last of which would eventually become one of the most important commodities to come out of India due to its use in gunpowder. However, this was at the time considered a minor achievement. At this point, the East India Company's Court of Directors had its sights on Southeast Asia rather than India, seeking to gain a foothold in places like Sumatra in order to compete against the Dutch spice trade there. These efforts were small in scale and not very profitable. A few outposts, known as factories, were established in Sumatra and other islands in the Indonesian archipelago, but these were closed down by the Dutch. Japan and China both stood out as highly desirable trading partners, but Europeans had little success there in the 17th century; Japan's Tokugawa Shogunate closed the country to all foreign traders except a handful of Dutch merchants, while China allowed foreign trade under highly controlled circumstances. In short, the major Asian empires still controlled most of the trading activities in the region. Even among European powers, the East India Company lagged behind the VOC and the Spanish Crown, which controlled the Philippines (Marshall, 490-91).

The East India Company's fortunes began to change in the early 18th century. Around 1700, East India Company merchants redirected their attention to India and established factories in several major cities, most notably Calcutta. These factories produced immense quantities of textiles and spices. In the 1720s, the profits of the East India Company finally exceeded those of the VOC as the British began to pull ahead of their European competitors in Asia. From this point on, the economy of Britain, its North American colonies, and Western Europe as a whole became heavily intertwined with Indian trade (Marshall, 490-91).

In the 1700s, India was ruled by a number of princes kept in power by mercenary forces. It was the norm then, and not the exception, for the British East India Company, which had growing interests to protect in Madras, Calcutta, and Bombay, to employ Indian soldiers for their cause. Unlike many other proprietors, the Company had a reputation of paying on time and without fail. As an attractive employer, the British East India Company would eventually come to dominate large parts of India, not with Anglo armies–which amounted to only 10% of the Company force–but with Indians: "It was, in other words, an Indian army that conquered India for the British."[9]

This is not to say all relations between Indians and the Company were friendly. It must be remembered that in the mid-1700s, the British were not building an unchallenged empire as

---

[8] Ibid.
[9] Ibid., 12.

many modern historians paint it, but actually competing with rivals for economic dominance. The British had built Ft. William in Calcutta as a defense against the rival French East India Company.

The East India Company's approach to India also changed dramatically in the 1740s. Where East India Company merchants had once been content with small outposts and factories in Mughal-controlled territories, where they had once thought more of profit than of territory, they began to act more as agents of imperial expansion. The reasons behind this shift are complex, but one major factor was the outbreak of the Seven Years' War. The Seven Years' War, considered by some historians to be the first truly global conflict, featured warfare between Austria and Prussia in Europe and their allies, and the French and the British in the colonial theaters. The war reached the Indian Ocean in 1744 when naval battles erupted between the French and the British. Two years later, war broke out between two Indian rulers: the Nawab (a term roughly equivalent to governor or provincial ruler) of Arcot, a British ally, and the Nizam of Hyderabad, a French ally. Operating largely as a proxy war between the two European powers, the conflict had a severe and negative impact on the local population.

At the war's end, the Nawab of Arcot stood victorious but saw his status reduced to that of a client state of the East India Company (Marshall, 492). Thus, the East India Company began to assert itself as a major figure in Indian politics and conflicts between different regional authorities. These changes coincided with similar changes in approach in the Dutch and French empires, with the new imperial turn in India coinciding with colonial efforts in Indonesia and the Pacific. Since many of the East India Company's choices abroad were driven by competition with other European states, it comes as no surprise that all of the major European powers adopted similar tactics.

In 1756, war broke out again, this time between the East India Company and the Nawab of Bengal. During the course of the fighting, 146 prisoners were locked, at the nawab's orders, in an 18 by 14-foot cell inside the fort, resulting in the death of nearly 50. The reports of the infamous "Black Hole of Calcutta" in lurid detail by British writers, created an anti-Indian fervor throughout Britain and affirmed the superiority of Anglo rule as necessary for the civilization of the country in the British mind.[10]

---

[10] Richard Cavendish, "The Black Hole of Calcutta." *History Today* Volume 56. Issue 6. June 2006.

A contemporary depiction of the Nawab of Bengal

# Depictions of soldiers at the battle

As trade within India increased in volume and value, the stakes for political control grew greater. The British, still reeling from the events of 1756, believed it necessary for their own defense (physical and economic) to have Company-friendly rulers on the thrones in areas of trade, and the Company involved itself in an Indian political dispute in Bengal to ensure such an outcome. It was, as St. John reminds his readers, not the "conquest of Bengal as such. The extension of British power occurred via the East India Company and proceeded in piece-meal fashion over several years. Even then it was not initiated with this end in view, followed no preconceived plan, and was certainly not endorsed by politically-conscious opinion within Britain. What…drove events forward were the actions of a few "private enterprise imperialists" motivated by the prospect of monetary gain. These men, also, possessed no plan and were drawn into the vortex of Bengali politics by sectional interest groups who wished to utilize the military services of the Company in their own power struggles…"[11]

Rather than a planned "conquest," the British operated on a "principle"—"it was permissible to use force to reconfigure the internal politics of Bengal if this appeared the path of greatest net benefit to the Company. The interests, rights, and attitudes of Indians themselves were an irrelevance."[12]

While historians typically mark the Battle of Plassey in 1757 as the true starting point of British rule in India, resistance continued in various forms. Peasant revolts and uprisings, while never successful in driving out the East India Company and their local representatives, occurred with regularity. In 1783, a massive peasant uprising in Rangpur took control of entire regions for over a month, going so far as to elect their own government and replace the old ruler with a new Nawab. East India Company officials brutally suppressed the uprising, which had consisted of men and women from a large cross-section of Rangpur society. At the direction of the East India Company, soldiers put down the revolt by killing civilians without trial. Subsequent peasant revolts erupted throughout the early 19th century. Most of these revolts began as a response to the economic strain of production quotas and tax collection. While some succeeded in inflicting violence and destruction on the East India Company and its local representatives, peasants were never able to form a coalition with which to engage in sustained fighting (Sen, History Modern India, 84-85). Riots and rebellions would erupt, swiftly overtake a region, and then burn out or face opposition once they reached the neighboring province.

Elites continued to engage in more organized military resistance. The most notable of the post-Battle of Plassey figures to challenge East India Company rule was heir to the kingdom of Mysore, Tipu Sultan, who engaged in a series of four wars against East India Company incursions into his kingdom, conflicts collectively known as the Anglo-Mysore Wars. Tipu

---

[11] Ian St. John, 19.
[12] Ibid., 19-20.

Sultan was notable for his extensive efforts to assemble an international coalition to oppose British influence in South Asia but despite his best efforts, he was killed in battle in 1799. This is generally considered the last serious attempt to check British expansion across the Indian subcontinent (Roy, War, Culture, and Society, 87).

**A depiction of Tipu Sultan**

**A painting depicting the death of Tipu Sultan at the Battle of Seringapatam in 1799**

## The Sepoy Rebellion and the End of the East India Company

British governance in India before the Raj is not easily explained. Regional differences and changing circumstances make simple description difficult, but a good general rule of the period is to understand that the East India Company was given major leeway to govern by the British crown. But all along, as the ultimate authority over English businesses interests and citizens overseas, the British government was within its rights to rule far more directly; it was merely content to allow the Company to work out its own governing policies, sharing power with local and regional Indian authorities.

In Bengal, the region where the rebellion that would change British-Indian relations permanently took place, the Company shared power with a local nawab. The Company was given increasing responsibility, including the power to collect taxes, or Diwani,[13] in 1773. Many have criticized this "Dual Authority" of both local Indian rulers and the rule of Company officials as allowing for greater corruption and creating anger and resentment throughout Bengal.[14]

---

[13] Percival Griffiths, The British Impact on India (London: MacDonald, 1952), 77.
[14] Ibid., 143-7.

Though a defender of Britain's contributions to India's history and economy, Kartar Lalvani calls the Company's collection of the Diwani "short-sighted greed" and charges the Company with a "horrendous blunder concerning the role of revenue collection."[15]

To the Indian people, the events of 1857 are known as the first War for Independence. For the British, the time is referred to as a mutiny, an uprising, or a rebellion.[16] It is ironic that a similar story played out just under 100 years earlier, during the American Revolution, or as the Americans called it, the War for Independence.

Whatever the moniker, in 1857, one of the Indian armies, the Bengal, mutinied. [17] In the most cursory histories of the period, the cause of the rebellion is simply cited as an oversight, a change in the type of grease used in powder cartridges rumored to contain animal fat. This revelation horrified both Hindus and Muslims. The British response, which either failed to recognize the need to address the growing rumors or attempted to force Muslim and Hindu soldiers to use the ammunition despite their objections, made things worse. Author John McLeod explains that though the controversy over animal-greased rifle cartridges was the immediate cause of the conflict, economic, religious, and political resentment existed and had been worsening throughout 1856.[18] He also argues that rather than the uprising being attributable to either one incident or one cause - such as concerns over attempts at religious conversion by Christian officers, anger at the British in general, or frustration over specific tax policies - the rebellion was fueled not only by those with specific complaints against the British, but by those who sought to end up on the right sight of history. McLeod argues that many Indians joined the rebellion only after the tide seemed to be turning in favor of Indian rebels: "In general, the deciding factor was whether or not such leaders felt that their interests and those of the people under their command would be best served by ending British rule."[19] McLeod concludes that the basis of the mutiny was ultimately economic, observing that "the commercial and educated classes of Calcutta, Bombay, and Madras had prospered under Company dominance, and held back."[20]

The rebellion was filled with internal conflict and rivalries among various groups, but one would be hard-pressed to find an author who does not cite the uprising of the Bengals as a turning point in British-Indian relations.[21] Though the cartridges greased with animal fat were withdrawn from service almost as quickly as they had appeared, the damage had already been done. The newly issued rifles required these cartridges to be opened with teeth prior to being jammed in the barrel of the rifle.[22] Long-term resentment toward British expectations and

---

[15] Ibid., 10.
[16] John Keay, India: A History. New York: Atlantic Monthly Press, 2000. 437.
[17] John McLeod, The History of India (Westport, CT: Greenwood Press, 2002), 81.
[18] Ibid.
[19] John McLeod, The History of India (Westport, CT: Greenwood Press, 2002), 82.
[20] Ibid.
[21] John Keay, 437.
[22] Ibid., 438.

demands boiled over since "to cow-reverencing Hindus as to pig-paranoid Muslims the new ammunition could not have been more disgusting had it been smeared with excrement; nor, had it been dipped in hemlock, could it have been more deadly to their religious prospects."[23] Rumors about the British "tricks" spread quickly, as did resentment and mistrust.

An estimated 80,000 Indians and over 5,000 British were killed during the rebellion, often horrifically. As British historian Percival Griffiths said of the rebellion in retrospect, "It is useless to pass judgment on these excesses on both sides. Cruelty begets cruelty, and after a certain stage of suffering and horror justice and judgment give way to the demand for vengeance. All that can be said is that both amongst Indians and English the Mutiny brought out the best and the worst."[24]

Once it had put a stop to the rebellion by defeating the various Indian rebel groups individually,[25] the British government end up ruling India directly. However, as McLeod pointed out, "Like much of British imperial expansion, taking formal control of India was not intentional. Instead when British lives and trading interests (represented by the East India Company) were threatened by violent reaction to encroaching westernization, London felt obligated to step in to take control of both the situation and the country."[26] The news was delivered to the Indian people in a proclamation by the English government in 1858.[27]

At the highest levels, the new administrative structure of India was out of the new India Office and headed, at home, by the Secretary of State for India. In India, a new title–viceroy–was added to the position of governor-general, signifying that the authority now held the weight of the crown.[28]

Why did the British desire to continue their reign in India despite the bloody rebellion of 1857? McLeod cautions against a too ready acceptance of any single purpose. Rather than seeing India as a purely economic venture or only a source of international empire, the British desired to keep India within the empire for multiple and changing reasons. Certainly, there were economic benefits for Britain, as 25% of Indian taxes ended up in the mother country for administrative purposes, retirement pensions for former Indian officers, and as interest on loans made to India.[29] Acknowledging the economic factors, however, should not allow for the discounting of others, including Britain's desire to maintain her holdings in the East; to influence India religiously, educationally, and culturally; and to maintain her own image as a dominant power.[30]

---

[23] Ibid.

[25] John McLeod, 83.
[26] Robert Carr, "Concession & Repression: British Rule in India 1857-1919: Robert Carr Assesses the Nature of British Rule in India during a Key, Transitional Phase," *History Review*, no. 52 (2005).
[27] Sneh Mahajan, British Foreign Policy, 1874-1914: The Role of India (London: Routledge, 2002), 37.
[28] McLeod, 83.
[29] Ibid., 84.

Though the proposal was raised far earlier in 1858, it was not until 1877 that Queen Victoria was named the "Empress of India," in a ceremony held in Delhi.[31] The interest in expansion of nations like Russia, Austria, and a relatively new German nation-state eager to make a reputation, led Victoria to believe the title of empress would raise her status from "petulant widow to imperial matriarch."[32] These "psychological" concerns must weigh as heavily as the economic ones in understanding the desire for continued British dominance of India.

**Queen Victoria**

---

[30] Ibid.
[31] Sneh Mahajan.
[32] Ibid.

**A formal portrait of Victoria as Empress of India**

**An Indian coin depicting the queen**

Though it had been decided that the rule of India would continue under the Raj, the way in which the relationship between Britain and India would be viewed had yet to be determined. For many British thinkers, the mutiny "left a lasting mark on both the style and the ideology of British rule."[33] Though the liberals believed India could be westernized and modernized through a combination of education and political cooperation, based on "the gratitude and appreciation of the ruled…These beliefs had proved to be illusions."[34] Instead, the bloody mutiny confirmed in the minds of many Brits that India was and would remain a group destined for Western subjugation, ruled, albeit benevolently, by racial superiors. Albertini and Wirz explain, "This was henceforth the ideological basis of the British Raj. Although the other things the English brought India—domestic peace, a unified legal system, and modern administration—were also considered to legitimize British rule, the implicit or stated conviction remained, that India now "belonged" to England and that Indians were incompetent to rule themselves or manage their own affairs; as indeed were all nonwhite races."[35]

The India Office understood the need to avoid another rebellion, and they also knew that to rule British India effectively, it must have the support of nearly the whole land. Thus, the British increased the presence of British officers in India, but also concentrated on making alliances with Indian rulers in non-British regions of India, who were guaranteed their lands would never be annexed by the Crown in return for their loyalty. In its 1858 Royal Message, it was declared "that the British 'desire no extension of [our] present territorial possession and would respect the rights, dignity and honour of the native princes as our own.' States and territories, large and

[33] Rudolf Von Albertini and Albert Wirz, European Colonial Rule, 1880-1940: The Impact of the West on India, Southeast Asia, and Africa, trans. John G. Williamson (Westport, CT: Greenwood Press, 1982), 7.
[34] Ibid., 8.
[35] Ibid.

small, that had come under British rule during the expansionist phase as a result of protectorate and subsidiary treaties, retained the same status."[36] Those who had remained faithful to Britain during the rebellion were highly rewarded.[37]

To aid in the rule of the Indian people, the British established a new Indian Civil Service with a dedication to maintaining and promoting fair policy and rooting out corrupt practices.[38] The Civil Service employed British officers, but also many Indian civil servants who worked in India's provinces. The officers were described by one British-Indian writer as "minutely just, scrupulously honest, and inflexibly upright, introducing the culture and tradition of impartial and good governance without corruption."[39] The Indian Civil Service, which commentator after commentator mentions as an astounding example of fair and peaceful rule of many by the few, soon became known as "the steel frame" of India.[40]

**The New India**

**A depiction of Viceroy Lord Canning meeting Maharaja Ranbir Singh of Jammu &**

[36] Rudolf Von Albertini and Albert Wirz, European Colonial Rule, 1880-1940: The Impact of the West on India, Southeast Asia, and Africa, trans. John G. Williamson (Westport, CT: Greenwood Press, 1982), 12.
[37] McLeod, 85.
[38] Kartar Lalvani, *The Making of India: The Untold Story of British Enterprise*. (London: Bloomsbury Continuum, 2016), 13.
[39] Ibid., 14.
[40] Ibid.

### Kashmir in March 1860

The office of Secretary of State for India was a new one for Britain. The secretary's office was located in London, and the name of his department, the India Office.[41] The Sepoy Rebellion of 1857 had illustrated the horrors of widespread mutiny. As the British crown took over administration of the country, ratios were placed on the British Army which prevented the number of Indian soldiers to British from exceeding 3 to 1.[42] This proved difficult to enforce, as the expense of stationing and maintaining British troops overseas in these ratios was expensive.

[41] Percival Griffiths., 83.
[42] Pradeep P. Barua, Gentlemen of the Raj: The Indian Army Officer Corps, 1817-1949 (Westport, CT: Praeger, 2003), 3.

**The first Secretary of State for India in 1874, Robert Arthur Talbot Gascoyne-Cecil**

The debate over the long-term effects on the Raj continues today. Colonial India, it is said by critics, was little more than a storehouse of raw materials and a market for British goods and her world empire. Others argue that though there were long- and short-term problems with the Raj, the British should receive credit for some contributions to India's benefit. These include the establishment of law and order that led to greater domestic peace and the extensive civil administration system that allowed the country of 347 million to function. In its 1958 report on "The New India," the Planning Commission of the Indian government celebrated India's new found independence, but stopped short of critiquing their former colonial masters, claiming, "The British withdrew from India in a manner honorable to both sides and worthy of their own rich tradition of freedom, leaving a fund of goodwill and eagerness on the part of India to forgive and forget and to remember only the best of the past."[43] The "best," according to government officials, included a "strong administrative structure of the former Government," a highly trained and organized" Indian Civil Service, and "the judiciary and police system which had established both a mechanism and respect for law and order over the entire country."[44]

To rule such a massive country as India required an efficient administration and many bureaucrats to carry out the everyday work of governing. The Indian Civil Service, in its earliest form established in 1757, did just that. At first, the Indian Civil Service was dominated by Britons with only a few, narrowly selected Indians who had attended university in England and passed the Civil Service exams in London. Eventually, the Indian Civil Service became a home for aspiring classes of Indian professionals, who, after 1923, could take the Civil Service exam (though still in English) without leaving the country.[45] After passing the exam, however, ICS recruits spent time in Britain, taking classes and acquiring the "British social graces" necessary for service to the Crown.[46]

Members of the ICS had a remarkable amount of independence, charged with administering their assigned colonial areas with little interference or direct supervision after an initial period of training under a British officer. At only 25 or 30, a member of the service would carry out British policy, largely improvising their own responses to crisis or challenge, since communication was rare and difficult.[47] These young men, however, also carried out their role in a way that restored confidence in the fairness of the British, rejecting corrupt practices that had been in place under the East India Company, administering justice and settling disputes instead, while traveling a district on horseback.[48]

---

[43] Planning Commission, Government of India, The New India: Progress through Democracy (New York: Macmillan, 1958), 15.
[44] Ibid.
[45] Ibid.
[46] Ibid., 10.
[47] Ibid., 11-12.
[48] Ibid., 13.

In *Anglo-Indian Attitudes*, Clive Dewey chronicles the life and work of two Britons who dedicated their lives to service in the Indian Civil Service. He begins his work acknowledging it would likely draw criticism from opponents of British colonialism as well as those who believe that the presence of the British benefitted India. Dewey rejects the adoption of either position as legitimate when making judgment of the actions of individuals, choosing to "accept the possibility that ideas driven by the process of intellectual discovery direct our action by invading our minds."[49]

Dewey argues that within the Indian Civil Service were many men, who because of their childhoods, education, training, and actions, had an impact on Indian society that would be foolish for historians to ignore. Since the numbers of years of service for an ICS officer was 35, such men had more than enough time to shape the culture and policy in the areas in which they worked, often ruling over 300,000 people on their own.[50] There was, however, a divide in the ICS, which meant it "veered between...assimilation and preservation...between westernizers who wanted to change Indian and orientalists who loved it..."[51]

By the time India became independent, the 980-strong officer corps had over 500 native officers, many of who continued to serve through their 35-year commitment and beyond. The British ICS left the country, but not without misgivings, as one said in 1946: You want us to leave India. We would leave very soon but one thing you must remember that you would not be able to maintain those vaulting standards of fairness, honesty, efficaciousness and diligence in administration, which we maintained because of the conspicuous role of the ICS and other services despite difficulties of governing and numerous odds faced by us. Time would come when many of you would remember us with tears in your eyes.[52]

Under the crown, particular industries continued to flourish, though the lives of India's poorest did not dramatically change. About 70% of Indians remained agricultural workers. Those who entered businesses, those who grew crops that could be exported, and educated professionals saw great improvement in their economic status.[53] During the Raj, trade in both opium and indigo greatly declined, and new products–such as cotton, jute, iron, and wheat–began to dominate. Though much of what Indians produced brought about profit through export, some of these industries actually blocked out British products, as we will see below.[54]

Before the 1850s, cotton produced in India was largely exported to Europe for spinning or weaving. What was spun in India was completely by hand. The first steam-powered cotton mill did not reach India until 1856. Indians within the industry soon realized that their greatest profits

---

[49] Clive Dewey, *Anglo-Indian Attitudes: Mind of the Indian Civil Service.* (London: The Hambledon Press, 1993), viii.
[50] Ibid., 12.
[51] Ibid., 14.
[52] R.K. Kaushik, "The Men Who Ran the Raj." Hindustan Times. April 17, 2012.
[53] McLeod, 86.
[54] Ibid., 86-87.

could be made not in shipping raw materials to Europe, where it was difficult to compete, but in spinning in the new factories being built in India. The strategy worked. By becoming a leader in mechanized spinning, India beat out British competition and became the major supplier of yarn to China and Japan, as well as leading with 68% of domestic consumption. The addition of power looms in the 1880s meant more of the production process was kept at home. By the early 20th century, cotton textile production had become India's most important industry.[55] Unlike many other industries remaining in British hands, the cotton industry became truly domestic and is the best example of laissez-faire capitalism, which was the operant policy in India after the 1858 transition.[56] Gandhi would later condemn this westernization of India and call for a return to hand-spinning, both as a form of protest and salvation for India.

[55] Ibid., 86.

[56] B. B. Misra, The Indian Middle Classes: Their Growth in Modern Times (London: Oxford University Press, 1961), 215.

**Gandhi**

Railroad construction in India had begun before the Raj in 1850, and the first train operated in 1853.[57] The milestone of passenger transport was marked with great celebration as the British expressed the hope that "a well-designed system of Railways, ably and prudently executed, would be the most powerful of all worldly instruments of the advancement of civilization in every respect."[58] By 1861, there were over 1500 miles of railroad track completed. This number would be well over 40,000 miles by the late 1950s.[59] In his study of economic improvements under the Raj, I.D. Derbyshire, who rejects what he calls the "immiserationist" interpretation of

[57] Ian Kerr., *Engines of Change: The Railroads that Made India.* (Westport, Connecticut: Praeger, 2007), 5.
[58] Ibid., 6.
[59] Ibid., 10.

the Raj. He also argues that recent scholarship tends to support a "meliorist," or positive, view of British rule.[60] Derbyshire cites three factors in the improvement of Indian life and per capita income growth for the native population: a peaceful and well-administered government after 1857; the expansion of European markets for raw goods and easier access to these markets through technology; and the development of India's rail system.[61] The railways constructed in India brought many benefits, including commercial reliability. Rail helped to alleviate the effects of monsoon rains on trade prior to rail travel. Though weather affected trains, the flow of commerce was steadier during the days of land and river transport, and they could be shut down completely at times. River and land transport also faced challenges as a result of changes being wrought in India. Though riverboat carriage was the cheapest form of transport for goods, it was also "risky, seasonal…and excruciatingly slow."[62] These problems were exacerbated by the effects of canal building in India which lowered river levels and made transport of goods by river even more challenging in certain areas. Land transport via pack animals improved after the innovation of the bullock cart, but faced challenges similar to those of the riverboat.

**"The most magnificent railway station in the world." says the caption of the stereographic tourist picture of Victoria Terminus, Bombay, which was completed in 1888.**

Railway construction would change the Indian economy radically and permanently, especially in Western India. Railways provided a vital link between India's fertile and heavily populated Doabs (regions of great agricultural yield due to rich soils and heavy cultivation) and the port cities of Bombay and Karachi.[63] Though Indian nationalist writers often claimed the changes wrought by rail were responsible for the famines that periodically struck India during the Raj,

---

[60] Derbyshire, I. D. "Economic Change and the Railways in North India, 1860-1914." *Modern Asian Studies* 21, no. 3 (1987): 522.
[61] Ibid., 523.
[62] Ibid., 526.
[63] Ibid., 527.

Derbyshire rejects their claim that agricultural production shifted from grains and subsistence farming to a singular focus on cash crops for exports such as sugar, indigo, and cotton. Instead, he claims rail and the accompanying lower shipping rates, as well as the opening of the Doabs to western ports, allowed production of both domestically consumed grains and cash crops to increase "in tandem."[64] Grain production, he states, actually increased, from 57,000 tons in the years between 1880-1884 to over 560,000 tons in the years prior to World War I. While some of the increase was shipped overseas to newly opened export markets, over 300,000 tons of grain during this period were shipped inward and consumed domestically.[65] Grain production was mixed with the production of crops that helped to restore the soil and allow for year-round production.

Rail also changed the traditional practices of Indian rural areas. It had been common practice for villages to build grain storage facilities and to store up the excess for protection against crop failures. While this storage had often saved lives in earlier times, the implementation of cheap rail transport made this type of grain storage obsolete. Grain could go immediately to market to meet the demand, and where disaster struck, rail allowed a targeted response. Comparing two periods of short supply, the 1860 crop failures (when rail access was still limited), saw famine conditions even with a transport of 175,000 tons of grain to affected areas. Similar conditions in 1907 were alleviated with 725,000 tons of grain shipped by rail.[66]

While Derbyshire's work rejects the overall claim that the rich grew richer and the poor grew poorer as a result of the Raj and rail, he concedes that the development of West Indian farming led to a decline for agricultural workers in the East. At the same time, he notes that rail benefitted eastern regions by creating cheap transportation opportunities for East Indian workers who found employment in the Jute mills.

The number of people who were transported by rail in India grew each year. In 1920, 175 million Indians traveled by train somewhere in the country.[67] The railroad also became one of the three largest employers of the Indian population, just behind the Indian Army, the post, and telegraph. Today, the railroad continues to employ 1.6 million Indians.[68]

British innovations, particularly in rail, Derbyshire claims, were not the direct cause of the negative impact nationalist writers often claim. While those critical of the Raj's impact would cite slowed population growth, famine, decreased native land holdings, and the decline of the handicraft industry as evidence, more recent scholarship indicates these problems were more localized and offset by gains in other areas. Though both sides would agree the more

---

[64] Ibid., 530.
[65] Ibid.
[66] Ibid., 532.
[67] Ritika Prasad, *Tracks of Change: Railways and Everyday Life in Colonial India.* (Daryaganj: Cambridge University Press, 2015) 2.
[68] Kartar Lalvani, 21.

independent, middle-class farmers and upper classes benefitted much more and at a faster rate than the poorest agricultural workers, meliorists claim the negative impact of rail was the result of already existing poor hygiene which spread more quickly and easily as a result of rail transport. Derbyshire cites Gandhi on the matter, recalling his statement regarding "the protection of natural segregation was trenched upon and India was opened up to a scourge of disease such as South America had been in the 16th century."[69] He reminds his readers that cyclical famine as a result of crop failures was a part of Indian life, well before British rule, and in fact, that the impact of famine was greatly reduced post-1900 by the very existence of rail.

Of the four charges nationalist historians hold against the British, Derbyshire credits one: the decline of the handicraft industry. As far as the other charges, he exhorts the student of Indian history to consider the economic motives of the writers who were often the best-educated Indian natives, hailing from Bengal. It was, Derbyshire contends, the opening of prosperity to those in the lower classes and castes that influenced these writers to view the continuing changes as harmful. Having experienced the benefits of favorable relations with the British East India Company, they were loath to see opportunities open to all of India and not just to a select few. Additionally, Derbyshire calls his readers' attention to the conditions under which critical writing was undertaken, pointing out that during times of famine (in works he calls "gloomy"), the conclusions of nationalists were far more condemning of the British than during times of prosperity.[70]

In the final assessment of the benefits of British rail and accompanying economic change during the Raj, Derbyshire insists the division between those who condemn the Raj as negative and those who believe it benefitted India, results primarily, not from a difference in the data considered, but in the question asked. For nationalists, the question is: "Why did India not achieve takeoff?" asked in light of "their disappointment with comparative growth and income trends between India and Europe." For "meliorists," the question is instead: "Did per capita income rise between 1860 and 1920?"[71] He suggests that a middle ground, recognizing both significant growth and the limitations of that growth compared to other parts of the world, provides the most accurate accounting.[72]

**Women and the Raj**

In the wake of modern innovations and easier transport, British women began arriving in India in high numbers. The interaction between British women and the Indian people was largely relegated to inside British bungalows, removed from the crowded and busy living conditions of the Indians in Bombay, Calcutta, and Madras.[73] British ladies who often came to India to

---

[69] Derbyshire., 539.

[70] Ibid., 543.

[71] Ibid., 544.

[72] Ibid.

[73] Margaret Macmillan, Women of the Raj: The Mothers, Wives, and Daughters of the British Empire in India.

accompany their military husbands were called masters' women, or memsahibs.[74]

Margaret Macmillan's work on the lives of the women of the British Raj provides great insight as to their role in keeping British culture alive in the midst of a foreign and sometimes intimidating land. Though Macmillan often critiques British women for their lack of knowledge of the language, their assumption of superiority, and for "the greatest of all their incivilities...simply ignor[ing] India,"[75] she does not allow the modern perspective to prevent her from telling the story of the Raj. Instead, she cautions "to bundle them all up...into the stock figure of memsahib is to do to them what they did to the Indians."[76]

Certainly, life in India was far different than it would have been for the typical British woman. Whereas at home, most of the women would have been decidedly middle class, as representatives of the great British empire, they were expected to entertain and to take part in the "pomp and gaudy pageantry"[77] the Indians were taught to expect. To entertain at the expected level, the average British household in India might have 16 servants, each with specific tasks to carry out.

British women in India were used to living with an ever-present fear of mutiny. The history of the Sepoy Rebellion and simple recognition of the ratio of British to Indians made the fears real. As one woman wrote, "I honestly confess that the overwhelming crowds of people frightened me...What were we in the land, I thought, but a handful of Europeans at best, and what was to prevent these myriads from falling upon and obliterating us, as if we never existed?"[78]

Though British women had legitimate fears living in India, they faced little of the daily struggles the majority of Indian women met feeding their families, protecting them from disease, and navigating the changing face of Indian culture.

That changes to the suttee (the practice of immolating oneself after the death of a husband), the remarriage of widows, polygamy, and the general status of women both inside and outside the home wrought under British rule cannot be disputed.[79] The reason for these changes is still under debate by historians. The traditional view held that British changes to the law—outlawing suttee, legalizing and promoting second marriages for Indian widows, and the British education of women–were largely responsible for the change. Some modern historians claim that the changes in women's roles were driven by upper-middle class Indians who aspired to the British way of doing things, "attributing the changes to a desire to emulate Victorian moral codes and aping a bourgeois form of companionate marriage."[80]

---

(New York: Random House Trade Books, 2007) 23.
[74] Ibid., xi.
[75] Ibid., xii.
[76] Ibid., 12.
[77] Ibid., xxii.
[78] Ibid., 23.
[79] Ibid.

In fact, early British colonial policy in India instructed British courts to apply family law differently than in the rest of the legal code. Specifically, because of unfamiliar and centuries-long practices, such as infant and child marriage, British authorities in India were instructed to apply Hindu law to Hindu family disputes and Muslim law to Muslims. Early on, the concerns of the British East India Company were economic, and they opposed interventions they believed would negatively affect their profits. This was one of the reasons the Company opposed the entrance of Christian missionaries to India–something they were able to prevent until 1813, when the Company's charter was up for renewal.[81] It was only over time that the British changed their approach and began to directly intervene through legislation and practices designed to change the status and state of Indian women.[82]

British statesmen were convinced of the evils of Hinduism, calling it "the most enormous and tormenting suspicion that ever harassed and degraded any portion of mankind."[83] William Wilberforce and others considered introducing missionary efforts and Christian morals one the "greatest of all causes."[84] Gradually, the legal age of marriage was raised from ten in 1860 to twelve in 1891. The Hindu and Muslim populations resisted these changes, disputing the colonizers rights to intervene in private and religious matters, which were areas that had traditionally been left to Indians to regulate themselves. Rather than fight the legalities, the British chose to restrain the practices they believed were wrong than outlaw them completely. In 1929, the Marriage Restraint Act set criminal penalties for child marriages where the girl was under 12 or the boy under fifteen years of age.[85] John Keay takes a highly skeptical view of the reformers' motives and is critical of British attempts to eliminate customs such as suttee, which he claims were practiced rarely and not particularly linked to the Hindu faith.[86] He contends that with the introduction of the Christian mission, the British "became increasingly imbued with a sense of divine mission, their earlier toleration and even support of Indian religions evaporated, their conviction of Christianity's moral superiority grew, and their solicitude for the taboos of their subjects was eroded by carelessness and ignorance."[87]

The word, suttee, is, in fact, an English term used to describe the tradition in which an Indian wife would be burned to death in honor of her husband upon his funeral pyre. If a woman were pregnant at the time of her husband's death, or she was informed of his death after his body was disposed of–such as during wartime–the widow would be burned separately, with some personal item of his clothing as a symbol of his presence.[88] The Indian word *sati*, or faithful, was the word

---

[80] Ibid.
[81] John Keay, 428.
[82] Domenico Francavilla,. "Interacting Legal Orders and Child Marriages in India." American University Journal of Gender Social Policy and Law 19, no. 2 (2011): 535-538.
[83] John Key, 428.
[84] Ibid.
[85] Domenico Francavilla.
[86] John Keay, 429.
[87] Ibid.
[88] Edward Thompson, Suttee: A Historical and Philosophical Enquiry into the Hindu Rite of Widow Burning.

used to describe the widow herself, not the practice, the origin of which is disputed even by modern historians.[89]

The suttee appears to have been submitted to–and even desired–by many Indian widows. Was this due to pure religious belief and in honor of the gods, because of tradition, or perhaps, as Percival Griffiths suggests, a way to avoid the life that Indian widows–who were prevented by law and tradition from remarrying–were destined? Griffiths contends that "the life of a Hindu widow was one of misery. She was expected to eat only one meal a day, never to sleep on a bed, never to wear attractive clothes, and indeed to enter on a life of renunciation…friends and relatives next join together in lamenting her widowhood, and finally make her sit on a small stool. Then, one of her nearest female relatives, having previously muttered some religious formulae, cuts the thread of the tali, the gold ornament which every married woman in India wears round her neck. The barber is called in, and her head is clean shaved. This double ceremony sinks her instantly into the despised and hated class of widows…Doomed to perpetual widowhood, cast out of society, stamped with the seal of contumely, she has no consolation whatever except maybe the recollection of hardships she has had to endure during her married life."[90]

Despite this, some Indians, and the majority of the British, opposed the practice of suttee, which was finally banned in Bengal, Calcutta, and Madras in 1829 and 1830, while India was still under the control of the East India Company. During this period, the Liberal party had taken control of the British government, and their perspective on the mother country's role in her colonies changed policy significantly.[91] The governor-general who banned the practice, Lord William Bentinck, attempted to use pressure and reward to promote the end of suttee throughout all of India, including those lands still controlled by Indian rulers. The practice itself was largely ended by 1850.[92]

---

(London: George Allan and Unwin Ltd., 1928), 15.

[89] Ibid.

[90] Percival Griffiths, The British Impact on India (London: MacDonald, 1952), 219.

[91] Rudolf Von Albertini and Albert Wirz, European Colonial Rule, 1880-1940: The Impact of the West on India, Southeast Asia, and Africa, trans. John G. Williamson (Westport, CT: Greenwood Press, 1982), 6.

[92] Ibid., 225.

**Lord Bentinck**

During the Raj, however, there were incidents of suttee reported by groups who desired to show their independence from the British or who wanted to return to the traditional ways. An incident often referred to as 'The Last Suttee," may show just how much the practice had changed as a result of British and Indian opposition by the 1860s. When Mahrana Surup Singh died, a call was made to his multiple wives to become sati in his honor. The stakes were especially high, it was said, since the particular tribe in question had never had a leader cremated without a faithful wife to follow him into the next life. None of the wives agreed to participate, however, and instead, a young servant girl was compelled by her brother to receive the "honor." The child, like many who "willingly" participated in suttee, was put under much psychological pressure by both family members and the crowds who came to see the ceremony, and was given drugs that would render her state less than rational.[93]  It should be noted that "every wife had, for the first time in the annals of Mewar, declined to die on such an occasion."[94]

Rudyard Kipling's famous poem, "The Last Suttee," was said to be based upon this incident, but in his romanticized version, the queen herself, disguised as "a North-bred dancing-girl," and

---

[93] Edward Thompson, 112-113.
[94] Ibid., 113.

too afraid of the fiery death of the pyre, asks her "brother" to kill her with the sword. Kipling records his version of events in the last moments of the suttee:

> He drew and struck: the straight blade drank
> The life beneath the breast.
> "I had looked for the Queen to face the flame,
> But the harlot dies for the Rajpoot dame–
> Sister of mine, pass, free from shame,
> Pass with thy King to rest!"

> The black log crashed above the white:
> The little flames and lean,
> Red as slaughter and blue as steel,
> That whistled and fluttered from head to heel,
> Leaped up anew, for they found their meal
> On the heart of–the Boondi Queen![95]

After 1858, suttee was rarely practiced, and often used as a show of defiance to English rule in pockets of resistance and tradition, though Edward Thompson, writing in 1928, insisted that "it would be easy to show that suttee, in one form or another, public or private and irregular, has occurred almost every year in some part of India between 1829 and 1913; and it probably will still occur, though at longer intervals."

---

[95] Rudyard Kipling, *The Collected Poems of Rudyard Kipling.* (Hertfordshire: Wordsworth Editions Limited, 2004),248-251.

## Education and Reforms in the Raj

**The University of Lucknow, founded by the British in India**

Why the moral concern for India? Were British attempts at reform in such matters really just another for and of subjugation? To answer the question in full, one must examine the period before the Raj, when the foundation for education of the Indian people was being laid.

In 1819, Lord Hastings wrote that there would be a "time not very remote when England will wish to relinquish the domination which she has gradually and unintentionally assumed over this country, and from which she cannot at present recede."[96] For many British officials, there was a desire to see the Indian natives educated and the understanding that that education would eventually lead to self-rule. Though sounding paternalistic to the modern ear, another British official wrote of the ultimate goal for India to achieve self-rule: "We should look upon India, not as a temporary possession, but as one which is to be maintained permanently until the natives shall in some future age have abandoned most of their superstitions and prejudices, and become sufficiently enlightened, to frame a regular government for themselves, and to conduct and preserve it. Whenever such a time shall arrive, it will probably be best for both countries that the British control over India should be gradually withdrawn. That the desirable change contemplated may in some after-age be effected in India, there is no cause to despair. Such a

---

[96] Percival Griffiths, The British Impact on India (London: MacDonald, 1952), 245.

change was at one time in Britain itself at least as hopeless as it is here. When we reflect how much the character of nations has always been influenced by that of governments, and that some, once the most cultivated, have sunk into barbarism, while others, formerly the rudest, have attained the highest point of civilization, we shall see no reason to doubt that if we pursue steadily the proper measures, we shall in time so far improve the character of our Indian subjects as to enable them to govern and protect themselves."[97]

The effects of a classical Western education, it was understood, would necessarily lead to Indian independence. For some British leaders, any other result was unthinkable. This was true, not only in the decision to educate the Indian people, but in the debate about whether or not Indian natives should be allowed to hold high offices in the British administration. "Are we to keep these men submissive? or do we think we can give them knowledge without awakening ambition? or do we mean to awake ambition and provide it with no legitimate vent? Who will answer any one of these questions in the affirmative? Yet one of them must be answered in the affirmative by every person who maintains that we ought permanently to exclude the people of India from high office. I have no fears. The path of duty is plainly before us, and it is also the path of wisdom, of national prosperity, and of honour."[98]

As a 26-year-servant of the Indian Civil Service, Romesh Dutt found it "ungracious" and "painful" to criticize British policy, but found a sound basis for doing so in the very education provided to him in the mother country. Dutt quoted John Stuart Mill to support his charge that the very idea Britain would rule India in an unselfish manner was insupportable: "The government of a people by itself has a meaning and a reality; but such a thing as government of one people by another does not, and cannot exist. One people may keep another for its own use, a place to make money in, a human cattle-farm to be worked for the profits of its own inhabitants."[99]

Lord Macaulay debated the direction of British education in 1835 before the British Parliament. He acknowledged the debate between those who believed the future of education should be conducted in the native languages of India (the Orientalists) and those who believed that English must become the official language of the empire (the Anglicizers), but sided with those that advocated English, believing that "it is impossible for us, with our limited means, to attempt to educate the body of the people. We must at present do our best to form a class who may be interpreters between us and the millions whom we govern, a class of persons Indian in blood and colour, but English in tastes, in opinions, in morals and in intellect. To that class we may leave it to refine the vernacular dialects of the country, to enrich those dialects with terms of science borrowed from the Western nomenclature, and to render them by degrees fit vehicles for

---

[97] Ibid., 246.
[98] Ibid., 247.
[99] Martin Deming Lewis, ed., Romesh Dutt. British in India: Imperialism or Trusteeship? (Boston: D.C. Heath, 1962). 5.

conveying knowledge to the great mass of the population."[100]

By the 1850s and after the rebellion in 1857, many leaders of the Raj opposed the idea of an education that would lead to independence.[101] Instead, they fought inclusion of natives in places of authority and believed that the education of Indians was wasteful at best, and likely dangerous. But as Percival Griffiths explains, by this time, the forces of Indian independence had already been planted and would come to fruition.[102] Whether or not the Brits of 1857 and beyond realized it, "India's new young leaders-in-embryo…learned from their early failures how better to appeal for justice, equality of opportunity, and fair play–British ideals they culled from the works of Milton, Macaulay, Mill, and Morley, which they memorized and articulated more eloquently than did most British officials."[103]

The debate over whether the education of the Indians would concentrate on Western literature and science, or be taught by Hindus and in Sanskrit, was overwhelmingly won by those who advocated the former as the best path for India to modernize. There were individuals and families, however, who continued to prize the learning of Sanskrit, the ancient language of the priesthood, even as most English-educated Indians were pursuing Latin.[104]

Many Indian families prized the idea of a Western education and sacrificed time, money, and effort in order to obtain one for their children, as "the conviction grew steadily stronger among literate families that English education was essential to future prosperity and status."[105] Though in the larger cities of Calcutta, Bombay, and Madras, obtaining an English education was a matter of only registering and paying, in more isolated areas of the country, or in areas where native rulers prevented the establishment of English schools, children often had to travel to school, and many left home and lived at English boarding schools in the large cities.

Despite the desire for a Western education, which most believed would greatly aid in the economic advantages for the family, some Indian families worried about their sons taking on Western ways of relating to family and family authority, rejection of Indian traditions, and their potential conversion to Christianity. Therefore, the missionary schools were sometimes avoided by conservative families who wanted to ensure there would be no pressure or influence to reject Hinduism or Islam.

For women, educational avenues were opened up by the British, even if modern historians

---

[100] Thomas B. Macaulay. Bureau of Education. Selections from Educational Records, Part I (1781-1839). Edited by H. Sharp. Calcutta: Superintendent, Government Printing, 1920. Reprint. Delhi: National Archives of India, 1965, 107-117.

[101] Percival Griffiths, 247.

[102] Ibid., 248.

[103] Stanley Wolpert, "A Mixed Legacy: From the Raj to Modern India," Harvard International Review 32, no. 4 (2011).

[104] Judith E. Walsh, Growing Up in British India: Indian Autobiographers on Childhood and Education under the Raj (New York: Holmes & Meier, 1983), 36.

[105] Ibid., 38.

"have been more critical of the gender perspective of these liberal reformers, attributing the changes to a desire to emulate Victorian moral codes and aping a bourgeois form of companionate marriage."[106] The reasons behind the desire to educate young Indian women may be many, but the results,–the elimination of the suttee, laws against the remarriage of widows, and female infanticide[107]–surely improved the lives of Indian women despite the motives of those calling for female education and reform.

   In 1906, the new Secretary of State for India, John Morley, met with Indian Muslims. He "was planning the most far-reaching constitutional changes that India had seen since 1858,"[108] reforms that included separate elections for Muslims in India and the platform for the creation of the All-India Muslim League.[109] Morley was an idealist, who, though he stopped short of believing that India should rule herself, had the desire to see many more Indians from the middle class taking part in her governance.[110] After meeting with Indian nationalists in London in 1906, Morley wrote to the Earl of Minto, India's Viceroy, saying, "Not one more whit than you do I think it desirable or possible, or even conceivable, to adapt English political institutions to the nations who inhabit India. Assuredly not in your day or mine. But the spirit of English institutions is a different thing, and it is a thing that we cannot escape even if we wished."[111]

---

[106] Tanika Sarkar, "Women in South Asia: The Raj and After," History Today, September 1997.
[107] Ibid.
[108] John McLeod, 98.
[109] Ibid.
[110] Colin Cross, The Liberals in Power, 1905-1914 (London: Barrie and Rockliff, 1963), 50.
[111] Ibid., 51.

**Morley**

**Minto**

What would become known as the Morley-Minto reforms had two aspects, the administrative and legislative, both of which operated on the underlying principle of including more Indians in governmental decision-making. To that end, the viceroy named an Indian to his cabinet for the first time, and Morley named two Indians to the London council.[112]

The fight for the rights of Indians would dominate the next 40 years of Anglo-Indian relations. One of the key aspects of the debate was whether Indians should seek to gain rights as a single and unified political entity, or whether the various groups in India (Hindus, Mulims, Sikhs, etc.) should seek to carve out rights for themselves by dealing directly with the British. Legislatively, Morley promised the Muslims voting rights, but his critics claimed that Morley's reforms "were so full of the idea of Communal elections that 'the very thought of India vanished from the Bill, to be replaced by consideration for the separate communities of Hindu, Mohammedan, Sikh, Mahratta, non-Brahmin, Indian Christian, Anglo-Indian and English'—that is to say, representatives to the Assemblies and elsewhere were to be elected, not as Indians, but as Hindus, Mohammedans, Sikhs, Christians, etc.; and not to serve India, their common country, but to serve primarily their own particular classes and religious sects."[113]

Morley's critics saw his reaching out to the Muslim minorities, not as a move toward equality

---

[112] Ibid.
[113] Jabez T. Sunderland, India in Bondage (New York: Lewis Copeland Company, 1932), 238.

of reform, but as a way to continue to divide the Indian people. Morley-Minto ensured, one critic said, that there would be no actual progress made for Indian self-government, at least for another decade.[114] Other critics saw the reforms as a minimal response to the inevitable development of Indian independence. These critics emphasize the growing influence of India's educated professional class and over 60 million Muslims, both of which represented a growing challenge to Britain's rule. Cynical about the motives behind the reforms, they claim Morley and Minto "were consistent with the governing principle of the Indian prince who consulted his notables in durbar while reserving his autocracy,"[115] citing WWI, not British political reforms, as the real harbinger of independence.[116]

Comment [AE]: should this b

### Critiques of the Raj and the End of It

For all the accomplishments of the Raj, many British and Indians alike offered criticism of the British policy in India. This critique did not always accuse the British of bringing no improvements to India, but instead, pointed out that the benefits that did come with the East India Company, and later with direct rule, were beneficial primarily to Westerners. In the short-term, many local artisans and craftspeople were put out of business, but in the long term, critics said, the harm was far more devastating, resulting in long-term poverty and destructive patterns.

Romesh Dutt, a Calcutta-born 26-year member of the Indian Civil Service, was educated in the West. Like so many exposed to a Western education, he eventually critiqued the very system that had employed him, and resigned his position to become a voice for Indian independence.[117] He commended the British for their contributions, which he lists as peace, Western education, a strong administrative government, and a pure justice system,[118] calling these "results which no honest critic of British rule in India regards without high admiration."[119] Nevertheless, Dutt offers much critique for Britain's economic approach in India, arguing, "it is, unfortunately, true that the East India Company and the British Parliament, following the selfish commercial policy of a hundred years ago, discouraged Indian manufacturers in the early years of British rule in order to encourage the rising manufactures of England."[120] Duff criticizes the British in three areas: their trade policies–which "crippled" India's manufacturing; their impressive, yet devastating, collection of a land tax; and their demand for interest on the debt owed by India to the mother country as a result of the 1857 rebellion.[121]

Another Indian writer, Kartar Lalvani, has written a book that seeks to defend Britain's record

---

[114] Ibid., 239.
[115] William Roger Louis, Andrew Porter, and Alaine M. Low, eds., The Oxford History of the British Empire, vol. 3 (Oxford: Oxford University Press, 1999), 444.
[116] Ibid., 444-5,
[117] Romett Dutt in Martin Deming Lewis, 1.
[118] Ibid.
[119] Ibid.
[120] Ibid., 2.
[121] Ibid., 5.

in India. As a 50-year resident of England, Lalvani claims to have been unable to find a single Brit who would name a positive aspect of the British governance of India. Without denying that Britain was guilty–as many other nations have been–of exploiting India for her wealth, Lalvani's perspective is that once the country passed out of the hands of the British East India company and directly to the Crown, the contributions were positive and should be judged fairly.[122] He states, "The indisputable fact is that India, as a nation as it stands today, was originally created by a small, isolated island nation. India has endured as a democracy and as a unified nation thanks to the all-important and fully functional infrastructure of an independent civil service and judiciary, a disciplined and apolitical army and a well-drilled and efficient police force, all developed by the imperial power. Of course, the labor was local, indeed skillful, and the indigenous cultures were ancient and sophisticated, but it is worth pausing to consider what India would be like today if the British had chosen to stay at home."[123]

Author of *Indian Tales of the Raj*, Zareer Masani, describes his encounters with those who had lived through the British occupation period. Many of them bristle at what they saw as the British "obsession" with the Raj period, believing that other periods and influences are a more significant story for modern India. Thankfully, Masani pressed forward to record the remembrances of those who had lived through the period, whether highly critical of the British administration, cooperative, or in strong support.[124]

In 1885, only four years before the birth of Jawaharlal Nehru, the Indian National Congress organized and began the path to Indian independence. Still in its infant stages, the Congress would not see its goal complete until 1947. The Congress and the young man who would come to dominate it endured a long journey, fraught with delays and opposition, until he became India's first independent prime minister.

In its early stages, the Congress acted as a training ground for India's newly educated and politically awakened young men to hone their leadership skills. Meeting initially during the Christmas season, they passed a series of resolutions for change in India's governance, demanding "greater access by Indians to positions of governmental power, fewer taxes, reductions in military expenditure, and compulsory elementary education."[125] Although the resolutions coming out of the Congress were often ignored by British officials, "India's new young leaders-in-embryo…learned from their early failures how better to appeal for justice, equality of opportunity, and fair play–British ideals they culled from the works of Milton, Macaulay, Mill, and Morley, which they memorized and articulated more eloquently than most

---

[122] John Preston, "The British Were Imperialist Brutes? No, Britain Made India Great (says an Indian)". UK Daily Mail, 17 March 2016.

[123] Kartar Lalvani, *The Making of India: The Untold Story of British Enterprise*. (London: Bloomsbury Continuum, 2016), 2.

[124] Zareer Masani, Indian Tales of the Raj. (Berkeley: University of California Press, 1987), 1-6.

[125] Stanley Wolpert, "A Mixed Legacy: From the Raj to Modern India," Harvard International Review 32, no. 4 (2011).

British officials."[126]

Jawaharlal Nehru was born into a well-off Indian family and educated at English boarding schools, where he received a classical education along with many of his contemporaries. While at Harrow, he was exposed to a biography of the Italian nationalist Garibaldi, a figure who captured his imagination and admiration.[127] His later admiration of the Irish Independence movement caused Nehru to come into conflict with his moderate father, who had put great stock in the Raj early on, and enjoyed the benefits of British favor.[128] His son, having graduated from Cambridge and studying to pass the barrister's exam, eventually embraced a similar lifestyle in London, despite his attraction to the more radical elements of the Indian independence movement and a growing resentment of discrimination, which he regularly experienced at University.[129]

**Nehru**

---

[126] Ibid.
[127] Benjamin Zachariah, Nehru (New York: Routledge, 2004), 17.
[128] Ibid., 21.
[129] Ibid., 27.

In 1912, upon his return to India to begin practicing law with his father, the Swadeshi movement was already well underway. Swadeshi, meaning "of our own country," encouraged the forsaking of British goods and the colonial lifestyle, a movement that Nehru's family rejected. Instead, his father purchased a British automobile, marking himself as a man interested in continued cooperation and loyalty to the British way of life, in the mind of his son. Nevertheless, Nehru remained a faithful son, marrying a Brahmin girl in a match arranged by his father.[130]

Nehru remained interested in Indian independence, and resented what he saw as the divide and conquer methods employed by the British—emphasizing the enmity between Muslim and Hindu populations and helping to form the Muslim League, which would fight for its own rights, rather than for the recognition of Indian rights as a whole. The 1916 Lucknow Pact, signed by both the Muslim League and the National Congress, brought Hindus and Muslims together, as well as helping to promote cooperation between the two opposing independence parties, one more radical, the other more moderate, in its demands for home rule.

It was there, at the Lucknow Conference, that Nehru first met Mahatma Gandhi. Gandhi had returned to India from South Africa in 1915, where he had campaigned for better treatment of Indian soldiers stationed there by the British.[131] After spending a year touring India, Gandhi began his non-cooperation movement, encouraging civil disobedience, specifically appealing to Indian peasants through his peasant dress and manner of speaking.[132] Nehru's biographer, Benjamin Zechariah, notes that at the time of their Lucknow meeting, Nehru was "unable…to relate to [Gandhi's] style."[133] Though Nehru's father had joined the independence movement (largely as a result of British persecution of those who called for it), the Nehrus believed the path to Indian independence lay in the hands of the upper-middle, educated class, not in embracing the cause of Indian peasants or support of the British during WWI.[134]

India supported the British and her victorious allies during WWI, sending 1.5 million soldiers to war, funded with Indian revenue. During the war, progress was made in domestic industry and many British exports were disrupted. These factors led many to believe that Britain would now take its promises regarding India's independence seriously. Despite some action–such as the Montagu-Chelmsford reforms, which moderates believed held hope for the future–many Indians believed that "the British were willing to leave India–but always tomorrow."[135] The British agreed to further training for Indian nationalists, but also claimed their immediate removal would lead to conflict between the Muslims and Hindus and a vacuum of power in the East that would destabilize the world.

---

[130] Ibid., 28.
[131] Ibid., 33.
[132] Stanley Wolpert.
[133] Zechariah, 33.
[134] Ibid., 33-4.
[135] Ibid., 35.

Along with reform and cooperation, the British became increasingly dedicated to putting down the radicals who demanded a timetable they were unwilling to give. This was to be accomplished, in part, by extending the Rowlatt Bills, allowing martial law in India during the war.

Gandhi responded by launching his first Indian Satyagraha,[136] a tactic he had used successfully in South Africa. The movement encouraged Indians to "court arrest,"[137] an idea Nehru also embraced, though his father did not. Father and son would be divided in their agreement over the tactics employed in pursuing justice for India. Gandhi's methods, in fact, continued to confuse the more established independence movement. The head of the Muslim League, Muhammad Ali Jinnah, also protested the Rowlatt Bills, but both the Muslims and Hindus in Congress believed "Gandhi's 'extreme program' attracted the inexperienced and the illiterate, and caused further division everywhere in the country."[138]

Gandhi called for a rejection of British custom, including the burning of all British clothing, a boycott of British goods, and the unity of Muslims and Hindus in the fight to repeal the Rowlatt laws. He advised his followers to conduct their protest openly and without resistance to arrest, believing the appeal to right and justice, rather than violence, would win the day. Gandhi's methods were considered both dangerous and offensive by many British officials, including Winston Churchill, who believed that any willingness on the part of the British government to negotiate with Gandhi would be interpreted as weakness. Churchill was offended by what he believed was a deliberate deception by the man he referred to as a "seditious middle Temple lawyer"[139] to engage the support of the Indian people against British rule: "Gandhi, with deep knowledge of the Indian peoples, by the dress he wore—or did not wear, by the way in which his food was brought to him at the Vice regal Palace, deliberately insulted, in a manner which he knew everyone in India would appreciate, the majesty of the King's representative. These are not trifles in the East. Thereby our power to maintain peace and order among the immense masses of India has been sensibly impaired."[140]

---

[136] Stanley Wolpert, Gandhi's Passion: The Life and Legacy of Mahatma Gandhi (New York: Oxford University Press, 2002), 99.
[137] Zechariah, 36.
[138] Wolpert, Gandhi's passion, 100.
[139] Ramachandra Guha, "Churchill and Gandhi", The Hindu Magazine. June 19, 2005.
[140] Ibid.

**Churchill in the early 20ᵗʰ century**

Gandhi's April 1919 arrest led to heightened tensions in India as violence broke out in response. Though Gandhi rejected the violence on his behalf as a violation of satyagraha, the British continued to see resistance to the Rowlatt laws and developed a growing fear of Indian revolt.

On April 13, in one of the biggest turning points in India's history, a gathering of unarmed celebrants at Amritsar, or Jallianwala Bagh, was fired upon by British soldiers under the command of Reginald Dyer. Over 400 were killed.[141] As the details of the massacre were

---

[141] Stanley Wolpert, *Gandhi's Passion*, 101.

discovered (initially Gandhi himself blamed the Punjabis and tended to believe the British were in the right), the event "effectively killed moderate opinion in India."[142]

**Gandhi in 1919**

Throughout the 1920s, as the non-cooperation movement gained strength and popularity thus endangering the status quo, Nehru, his father, and Gandhi were all in and out of jail. Gandhi, whether jailed or free, continued to be the force behind the movement which ebbed and flowed with his words. For example, when a protest grew out of hand and a building was burned to the ground with British police inside in 1922, Gandhi suspended the movement, stating that if independence came by violence, it proved the Indian people were not ready to deserve it.[143]

[142] Zachariah, 38.
[143] Ibid., 47-49.

Nehru turned to socialism as the liberating force for India, while Gandhi retreated to semi-seclusion to restore himself both physically and spiritually. Frustrated and angry at the delay in progress, Nehru angrily wrote to Gandhi: "What then can be done? You say nothing—you only criticize and no helpful lead comes from you."[144] Nehru's ultimate rejection of the non-violence movement and full conversion to communism was soon to come. Gandhi's biographer explains: "To hold such an idealist as young Nehru in check Gandhi knew that he would have to abandon his life of rural retreat, returning first to the hurly-burly of urban political chaos like that he had found so hateful in Calcutta, and then to the enforced solitude of long years behind British bars and barbed wire walls."[145]

Nehru had no faith in hand spinning, or the return to simpler and less Western times Gandhi advocated. He also considered Gandhi's ancient Hindu ideals outdated and impractical, if not reactionary. But by the end of the decade, Gandhi emerged once again, hoping to save India from Nehru's now-communist leanings (despite their sometimes strained friendship) and accomplish independence in both a political and spiritual sense.

In his most famous satyagraha, the Salt March, Gandhi encouraged millions of Indians to boycott British salt as he marched across the country to the sea. In explaining his reason for return and renewed leadership, Gandhi said, "At one time I was wholly loyal to the Empire and...sang "God Save the King" with zest...Finally, however, the scales fell from my eyes, and the spell broke. I realized that the Empire did not deserve loyalty...it deserved sedition...to be loyal is a sin...We get nothing in return for the crores of rupees that are squeezed out of the Country; if we get anything, it is the rags from Lancashire...It is our duty as well as our right to secure Swaraj. I regard this as a religious movement...Today we are defying the salt law. Tomorrow we shall have to consign other laws to the waste-paper basket."[146]

To Gandhi's surprise, he was not arrested during the salt march, but many of his followers were, as the movement rapidly expanded to include many previously politically sidelined women, whom Gandhi particularly called upon to participate on behalf of their children and households.[147] The march ended, but it served as a catalyst for mass civil disobedience, which filled the British jails to capacity and created its own momentum.[148]

The 1935 Government of India Act once again promised India independence, but insisted on retaining the ultimate rights of intervention and the special privileges for British companies and representatives who would serve in the new government under specially protected positions reserved for Indian minorities. In the face of this newest delay, Gandhi once again withdrew to a more spiritual role, and the division between he and Nehru–a division between the indiginests

---

[144] Stanley Wolpert, *Gandhi's Passion.*, 129.
[145] Wolpert, 133.
[146] Ibid., 145.
[147] Stanley Wolpert, Gandhi's Passion, 147-149.
[148] Stanley Wolpert, A Mixed Legacy.

who supported decentralized rule and a return to hand production and the moderns, who believed that a modern, industrial and socialist economy must be the pattern–was now permanent.[149]

When World War II was declared, neither Gandhi nor Nehru would agree to support the British cause without a guarantee of India's immediate independence. Only Minnah, the leader of the Muslim League, agreed to send Muslim Indians into the fight. This proved extremely important, for when the Muslims asked the British for their independence, it was granted by partitioning the country into India, as well as the new land of Pakistan. Minnah believed that by negotiating with Britain directly on behalf of India's Muslims, he would gain a better outcome for what he called the Muslim Nation: "The Mussalmans are not a minority. The Mussalmans are a nation....The problem in India is not of an inter-communal but manifestly of an international character, and it must be treated as such."[150] Thus, Minnah rejected Gandhi and Nehru's calls for cooperation with the country's Hindus and Christians against the British.

Despite the fact that Nehru was imprisoned in 1940 and Gandhi in 1942 (both for public speech against the war), the time for Indian independence was finally drawing near. Followers of both men carried on the fight. Soon after the war's end, Winston Churchill was replaced as Prime Minister by the Labour Party's Clement Attlee. The change in government came with a change in position on the Raj. Atlee announced that Britain would grant India independence no later than 1948.

---

[149] Zachariah, 81.
[150] Wolpert, Gandhi's Passion., 194.

**Attlee**

In June of 1947, the British issued the final plan for Indian independence, known as the Mountbatten Plan, also known as 3 June–Plan. The plan promised that India's states would be given the chance to be free from British rule and the British Commonwealth; that the land would be portioned into two countries, India and Pakistan; and that the British army would leave the country effective August 15, 1947. With that, the 90 year reign of the British in India had come to an end.

A fully comprehensive examination of the legacy of the Raj is difficult, if not impossible. For every positive contribution of the West to the East, a counter may be offered. The division amongst the Indians themselves and the continual wars that have plagued the region since independence could be argued the result of long-term British design and intention, or as the consequence of their leaving a vacuum of power in abandoning India too quickly. What is not under debate is the amount of influence the Raj had on Indian history, and for that matter, world history.

As Zareer Masani explains, "The secret of its success was that the British in India chose to colonise people and minds rather than territory. And the results, whether in administration, law, or education, proved far more enduring and pervasive than any policy of white settlement could have been."[151] Both the orientalists and the modernizers recognized the greatness of India and sought to harness it for their own purposes.

Despite his reputation as Britain's Imperialist poet, Rudyard Kipling's "We and They" reminds the reader of the short-sighted view that may be taken by both "East and West." Perhaps in partial answer to Lewis's question about the results of the Raj, there are historical realities that support both its destructive and creative tendencies. Ironically, the "imperial poet" compels readers to consider the divide as perhaps not as great as it appears:

FATHER, Mother, and Me
Sister and Auntie say
All the people like us are We,
And everyone else is They.
And They live over the sea,
While We live over the way,
But–would you believe it? –They look upon We
As only a sort of They!


All good people agree,
And all good people say,
All nice people, like Us, are We
And everyone else is They:
But if you cross over the sea,
Instead of over the way,
You may end by (think of it!) looking on We
As only a sort of They![152]

**Online Resources**

Other British history titles by Charles River Editors

Other titles about the British Raj on Amazon

**Bibliography**

Barua, Pradeep P. *Gentlemen of the Raj: The Indian Army Officer Corps, 1817-1949.* Westport, CT: Praeger, 2003.

---

[151] Masani., 7.
[152] Rudyard Kipling, 790.

Carr, Robert. "Concession & Repression: British Rule in India 1857-1919: Robert Carr Assesses the Nature of British Rule in India during a Key, Transitional Phase," *History Review*, no. 52 (2005).

Cavendish, Richard. "The Black Hole of Calcutta." *History Today* Volume 56. Issue 6. June 2006.

Cross, Colin. *The Liberals in Power, 1905-1914.* London: Barrie and Rockliff, 1963.

Derbyshire, I. D. "Economic Change and the Railways in North India, 1860-1914." *Modern Asian Studies* 21, no. 3 (1987): 522.

Dewey, Clive. *Anglo-Indian Attitudes: Mind of the Indian Civil Service*. London: The Hambledon Press, 1993.

Francavilla, Domenico. "Interacting Legal Orders and Child Marriages in India." *American University Journal of Gender Social Policy and Law* 19, no. 2 (2011): 535-538.

Griffiths, Percival. *The British Impact on India*. London: MacDonald, 1952.

Guha, Ramachandra. "Churchill and Gandhi", *The Hindu Magazine*. June 19, 2005.

Kaushik, R.K. "The Men Who Ran the Raj." *Hindustan Times*. April 17, 2012.

Keay, John. *India: A History.* New York: Atlantic Monthly Press, 2000.

Kerr, Ian. *Engines of Change: The Railroads that Made India.* Westport, Connecticut: Praeger, 2007.

Kipling, Rudyard. *The Collected Poems of Rudyard Kipling*. Hertfordshire: Wordsworth Editions Limited, 2004.

Lalvani, Kartar. *The Making of India: The Untold Story of British Enterprise*. London: Bloomsbury Continuum, 2016.

Lewis, Martin Deming ed., *British in India: Imperialism or Trusteeship?* Boston: D.C. Heath, 1962.

Louis, William Roger, Porter, Andrew, and Alaine M. Low, eds., *The Oxford History of the British Empire,* vol. 3 (Oxford: Oxford University Press, 1999.

Macaulay, Thomas B. Bureau of Education. Selections from Educational Records, Part I (1781-1839). Edited by H. Sharp. Calcutta: Superintendent, Government Printing, 1920. Reprint. Delhi: National Archives of India, 1965, 107-117.

McLeod, John. *The History of India*. Westport, CT: Greenwood Press, 2002.

Macmillan, Margaret. *Women of the Raj: The Mothers, Wives, and Daughters of the British Empire in India.* New York: Random House Trade Books, 2007.

Mahajan, Sneh. *British Foreign Policy, 1874-1914: The Role of India.* London: Routledge, 2002.

Masani, Zareer. *Indian Tales of the Raj.* Berkeley: University of California Press, 1987.

Misra,B. B. *The Indian Middle Classes: Their Growth in Modern Times.* London: Oxford University Press, 1961.

Planning Commission, Government of India, *The New India: Progress through Democracy.* New York: Macmillan, 1958.

Prasad, Ritika. *Tracks of Change: Railways and Everyday Life in Colonial India.* Daryaganj: Cambridge University Press, 2015.

Preston, John. "The British Were Imperialist Brutes? No, Britain Made India Great (says an Indian*)".  UK Daily Mail*, 17 March 2016.

St. John, Ian. *The Making of the Raj: India under the East India Company.* Santa Barbara, CA: Praeger, 2012.

Sarkar, Tanika. "Women in South Asia: The Raj and After," *History Today*, September 1997.

Sunderland, Jabez T. *India in Bondage*. New York: Lewis Copeland Company, 1932.

Thompson, Edward. Suttee: *A Historical and Philosophical Enquiry into the Hindu Rite of Widow Burning.* London: George Allan and Unwin Ltd., 1928.

Von Albertini, Rudolf and Wirz, Albert. *European Colonial Rule, 1880-1940: The Impact of the West on India, Southeast Asia, and Africa*, trans. John G. Williamson. Westport, CT: Greenwood Press, 1982.

Walsh, Judith E. *Growing Up in British India: Indian Autobiographers on Childhood and Education under the Raj.* New York: Holmes & Meier, 1983.

Wolpert, Stanley. "A Mixed Legacy: From the Raj to Modern India," *Harvard International Review* 32, no. 4 (2011).

Wolpert, Stanley. *Gandhi's Passion: The Life and Legacy of Mahatma Gandhi.* New York: Oxford University Press, 2002.

Zachariah, Benjamin. *Nehru*. New York: Routledge, 2004.

## Free Books by Charles River Editors

We have brand new titles available for free most days of the week. To see which of our titles are currently free, click on this link.

## Discounted Books by Charles River Editors

We have titles at a discount price of just 99 cents everyday. To see which of our titles are currently 99 cents, click on this link.

Made in the USA
San Bernardino, CA
16 July 2018